BETWEEN HERE AND NOW

STEEN ANDERSEN

*The author wishes to thank Professor Rory McTurk
for some adjustments of phrasing*

CONTENTS

I

HERE

The basement is full of secrets
there aren't any lights and a torch is of no use

the door leading to the steps is confusing
there's white coating and a brass handle
a keyhole abandoned for years

when it opens the other side is a cracked mirror
and messy flakes of paint

OUTSIDE

Bedtime stories are full of miracles and friendly animals
all of them frightening

especially in summer they're darkness
and from other worlds
half-heard children's voices tell me they're playing

through the window a view of clouds
always drifting the same way

A GAME OF OUR OWN

When the neighbours are abroad
we play our special game of hide-and-seek
round and round their house

I'm in the lead and count to ten as agreed
turning I don't see a soul
I count again and they run back in line behind me

they're all there
except for one who's no doubt round the corner

once more I count to ten, a bit quicker
hoping to see one of them turn up late

once more before I break our rules
and decide on the opposite direction

and they don't object because I count backwards

UP THERE

I only climb trees when I'm on my own
the weeping willow in the garden is reassuring
its green leaves hide my efforts

now and then I stop
to make sure the branches aren't too thin
and I check the distance from the ground

on my way down I mustn't look
instead I suddenly lean on the trunk
and look up to see where I was

the worst part is the dizzy longing
new views across hedges and fences
and the woods where I never climb trees

MY SECRET PLACE

My secret place is in the middle of the wood
where there are no paths or tracks
one day the trees will be thinned out

trains can only be heard when there's an easterly wind
traffic is too far off
the rustling of the leaves is silence

thick needles make the soil feel soft and warm

nobody knows about my secret place
I keep a few books there
and a skull bigger than a stag's

suddenly it's many months ago
and I can't find my way

DIRECTIONS

They're shooting a few scenes at the station
and the job takes hours
the script supervisor is busy all the time
the camera is moved about
and sunshine and cloudy weather are taken into account
six months later I buy an opening night ticket

during breaks they're relaxed and laugh
although a plot twist is round the corner
a couple of times shooting comes to a halt
as a train stops or tears along and seeing the film
I notice that the scene where the hero gets off
was shot at a different station
so he's in focus when he notices the people
who had expected to see somebody else

all of them are famous actors
why don't they need an extra
a boy kicking a football against a wall
I hear the director's words
and imagine myself returning to puzzled looks

I don't know where I'm coming from
or how long I've been away
but as long as the setting is real it isn't important
I'm not nervous at all
I carry a bag and a leather brief-case
a Leica on a strap
and say a few words to a boy with a football

THAT DAY

That summer I want to visit the other shore
a day of dead calm and when there's no wake of ferries

a bit north or south
so I'm out of sight when I set course

I make for a church or a house
figure out invisible currents
and check again and again after one hundred strokes

I need food and drink, an extra oar
and most important: a camera to confirm
how far I'm from the shore that I come from

I estimate distance and time frame
allow for tiredness and winds later on
I'm the only one in the boat
and afterwards I tell no one about my rowing

SCHOOL

The school gate is locked
I'm surprised as I'm always early

ringing the bell would be useless
looking at the front windows
I see a light in one of them

one of the parallel classes
I hardly know their names
there's always stiff competition
a lack of knowledge about their teachers
and I'm not aware of their timetable

as the gate slowly swings open
the only place I can go is their staring

an unclaimed desk
with a dried inkwell and a locked drawer

in front of the blackboard there's a map
of countries I've never heard about
rivers with no access to seas
and all borders are mountain ranges

PHOTOS

On my way to the airport I see a second-hand bookshop
where there used to be an estate agent
although I'm late I get off the bus
the only other bargain hunter scowls
maybe she thinks I'm looking for the same books as her

the good buys are too heavy for my cabin luggage
there's a table displaying faded postcards
most of them claiming Wish you were here!
there are also photos and suddenly three I recognize
childhood observing me in the strange surroundings

that's me! I tell the owner
who shrugs his shoulders unable to remember
where the pictures came from or when

once more I study the photos
seeing things I've forgotten and at the same time
the unlikely location removes me from myself
minutes postpone the purpose of my trip
and this evening's view of Lake Windermere

the three photos turn into a single question
while the owner wavers between hoping for a deal
and wanting to go home
the bargain hunter has left
no doubt with books that might give me the answer

THE FAMILY TREE

A few weeks after my mother's death
I find a family tree which she never mentioned
thirty photocopied pages
and on sheets of paper attached where relevant
the next bewildering generations in her handwriting

I see sets of siblings called names
that a few years ago would seem old-fashioned
in the early 1900s some of them emigrated
their descendants are listed as carefully
as those that stayed closer to home

I trace my relationship to some of them
my third cousins once or twice removed
or whatever the correct terms are
one of them is Renata Constanza Jensen
born in Buenos Aires four months ago

I've found no letters from correspondents
in her diaries there's not a word about updates
how many copies were there of the family tree
have other relatives carefully added names
so that I and my descendants exist elsewhere?

WHERE I USED TO LIVE

I ring the bell where I used to live
the door is opened by a woman
who finds my request intriguing

many years ago I forgot some envelopes
full of letters and diaries and photos

they may have been thrown away
but nobody would dream of my hiding-place
behind a panel

following her I recognize after forty years
the open fireplace and the staircase to the first floor

suddenly I know that the house will never be the same again
if I take away those envelopes

SPACE

Sleep is space
in dreams we meet again
long before it really happens

I tell her that the dead don't remember
therefore they can't forget

II

PATTERNS

A bird heading for its shadow on the lake
wanting to meet itself

June light and trees
where nearby voices become distant

maybe a pattern resembling
doors opening and shutting

SOMEBODY ELSE'S

It's so white that when somebody enters
it must be an operating theatre

I'm here before doctors and nurses
without knowing what's wrong with me

all sorts of medical equipment
protect me against danger

this is the place where I'm supposed to be
yes, I must have been told to turn up here

at this hour on this day
which seems to be somebody else's

THE LIGHT OF THE TREES

The light of the trees is time's entry and exit
September: summer's sounds and colours recalled
revealing the next scenario

a whiff of chill
only the wind's moments are the same
every day beginning a little earlier, ending a little later
as shadows fill the world

a place saved by past years
silence where voices on paths diverged
on their way to a beach and a bare horizon

OR EXILED

Land in sight
but no means of making out my position
clouds are far away
the sky is a reflection of the sea
and invisible stars are rocks on the seabed

the boat is heading for a roadless exile
where I'm not expected
but someone's in a doorway facing the sea

PATHS IN THERE

When the rain stops
paths are darkness surrounded by trees
the wind is someplace else

someplace else belongs to the wind

in dreams I know my memory was wrong
the same may be true for other people
without their dreaming about it

THE CANALS

The wind subsides with the sudden sound of winter
the sky as blue as a day in May
everything's back in an altered landscape

distance equals presence
there are blind lakes before canals appear

the boats are no longer here
and their masts were unstepped
for passage under unmanned bridges

WHITE SURF

White surf in my sleep
on my chart the points of the compass rose are tales
longitudes and latitudes demanding new bearings
travels end long before they begin

night's visions are windows
where summer is no longer than a winter's day
clinging to words about white surf

THE SHIP

The ship's a fascinating mixture
of modern cruise liners and ferries of the sixties

she doesn't belong here
there are lots of banks and shoals
but she seems to feel at home

only in daytime, never carrying lanterns
so it's impossible to find out where she is at night

she's too concrete to be real
and too astonishing to be a ghost ship

if I tell people about her they won't believe me
and maybe she'll head out for somewhere else

CATTLE

The same cattle in the same pasture
zooming is needed
the calves watch me
the cows don't stop chewing

the first day I just walked on
yesterday I stayed a bit longer

it's tempting to return in five minutes
but it wouldn't be fair
in Philipsen's paintings cattle are also stationary
and wonderfully blasé

Theodor Philipsen: Danish painter (1840-1920)

THE PAVILION

The pavilion's a few yards out from the bank
after the boards the door needs a push
before you enter a windowed hexagon

cracks in the floor, glimpses of water
a table and chairs, cobwebs
and through opaque glass a placid winter-grey lake

two watercolours are memories
in one of them the door is ajar
and timbers and glass are water shadows

the other is the interior of the pavilion
the sun shining through the windows
chairs and table perfect brushstrokes

the table's laid for coffee and cake
soon the door will be opened
and the three sisters and their husbands will enter

LATER

No dreams are remembered after troubled sleep
until later when they're resentful
that they were forgotten for a while

they wake up claiming that my memory plays a trick on me
there's a struggle between us

were the firs in the night darkness beyond glass
or were there gauzy white curtains?

and far away from the windows a boat
with the shadow sail of the moon

TRACKS

Heading for the ditches
that every autumn are blocked by twigs
so that flooding seems imminent
near tracks becoming invisible

one hour before the shoot and company's expected
on a clear day that fades
after the beating of wings shows prisms of time

OTHER PEOPLE

All those other people:
one of them passed me hurriedly
another one looked around
and checked a dated map

on the dusty road
the rest of them slowly led by a dog

his eyes burning
searching for me

A DRIVE

As I expected there are no other cars here
and I drive slowly in circles stepping on the brake pedal
as I suspect a malfunction

I hesitate before getting out
but having driven so far I don't want to return
since marked or nameless paths await me

I leave my mobile in the car
which I don't really want to lock
but of course it's silly to be careless

there's no way into the woods
I walk a full circle and only see solid foliage
there used to be seven paths to choose from

now the gravel road taking me here is also gone
no trees should spread so quickly and they all look old

I remember trees in my garden that I need to cut down
every time something worries me
for example the wind coming from the wrong direction

trees shooting up though they should have stopped growing
some people would call it hallucination
but it's no more hallucination than treetops swaying one way
when clouds and the neighbours' flags indicate the opposite one

a storm is gathering
soon it'll be dark

or the sun will go on shining
as words written in invisible letters

AGAIN

I don't really spend much time in airports
but surprisingly often I see old class mates and distant relatives

always after certain items on the agenda
security check
buying a bottle of single malt
choosing a restaurant
buying a newspaper
confirming the gate number and the time it takes to get there

next recognition and gracious surprise
questions about destinations
three-minute small talk

afterwards I go to the restaurant of my choice
study The Times waiting for my food
and I've already completed most of my journey

ARCHAEOLOGY NOW

Coming home from a trip I see a dig in the field
two archaeologists hard at work
two hundred yards from the fence

I make a habit of going out there once a day
where they uncover a grave
that so far is impossible to date

I don't really ask them how they're getting on
but I look at the dig and try to guess
and we talk about topography and the wood some distance away

now and then I look in the direction of my house
distance and viewpoint are puzzling
until I'm in the garden again

but I'm out there when tools and weapons appear
and the house vanishes

DOORS

They used to be in other homes
so the doors in this house are dissimilar

they link five rooms
whose functions were both obvious and vague

open spaces and in a bow window
a woman half-hidden

every time the door-frame was perfect
and only a single coat of paint was needed

so doors that had been locked or now and then were ajar
seem to have been here all the time

WIND

Against the wind
but suddenly I feel it behind me

it pushes me along
making my steps more difficult

a place never seen before
not even in dreams without a horizon

a picture in black-and-white

a scenery of hills and river
far away a mountain, it seems

the wind is scattered words
a language I'm supposed to have known long ago

gentle words out of context
telling me about somewhere else

NEIGHBOURS

Evening lights up street lamps
shadows unite

having keys to unlocked doors
it's easy to let other people get lost

they do it quietly
until they see new windows

I work out which houses they want to enter
they're death's neighbours

WINTER

In deepest winter
snowdrifts tear at rocks
and trees share their open light

BOOK OF DREAMS

Daytime incidents are never in my dreams
instead I enact my night visions
sometimes a walk is all that's needed
for instance to a park or a building
sometimes I have to look up addresses
and wait for a glimpse of acquaintances

if they're dead I visit their burial plot
taking a bunch of seasonal flowers
one approach is as good as the other
and some of those still living
would think I'm mad if they heard why I tracked them down

if dreams can't be remade
I take refuge to reading and pictures
getting hold of the relevant stuff is hard
but if I'm careless the incident recurs
in a much more difficult version
so it's better to do things properly without delay

I don't know about other people's habits
maybe I was close to an answer a few weeks ago
when a woman was looking at my house
somehow her face was familiar
and I realized that years ago we were lovers

I went to the window to rearrange a few photos
she looked relieved and left at once
maybe she deals with her dreams the same way I deal with mine
so far I haven't seen her at night
but to be on the safe side I now know where she lives
so I'm ready for what I may have to do one day

stuck between words and what's forgotten

LONGINGS

When everything seems to be in order
you may long for a place that's changed out of all recognition
where earlier years' faces turn away

GREEN SHADOWS

The boundary pines are felled
and memory escapes

you catch up with oblivion
where days disappear underhand

green shadows on the grass
when voices come together near the sundial

ONE FINE DAY

The houses are different
the people are the same and don't look a day older
they don't recognize me and most of them
shake their heads when I tell them my name

a few of them hesitate
and ask someone who's standing close to them
I give up saying what I came here for
and take refuge in the future to be a shadow

unique and my own in forgetfulness

ONCE UPON A TIME

Tell me more about your dead, she says
much younger than me

I try to remember
what she already knows

on my guard because she smiles
but my answer is straightforward

I think

III

ARRIVALS

Contrary to what I expect the front door is open
I see the passage and where it ends
another door to the rest of a house I used to know
I didn't enter all its rooms
some were off limits, others I shunned
thinking I'd find them eventually

welcome, she says
although she sounds sincere
she may have said the same thing to other people
or to me somewhere else
time is this place and therefore myself

I open another door
to find white curtains and windows ajar
I can no longer distinguish one room from the next
it's impossible to know which ones to enter
the click of the lock a few seconds later
is the distance to everything else

PASSPORT

Of course my passport is valid
nevertheless I get nervous
as they examine it so thoroughly
they even send for the police
and the queue behind me quickly lengthens

the check-in officer sends me an artifical smile
the fussy policewoman rubs the passport between her fingers
looks over the photo and me three times
apparently the lack of visas and stamps makes her suspicious
but she ignores me when I tell her about my travels

I wish I'd checked in before I left home
I wish there were more machines in the terminal
I wish I didn't have to go abroad

after talking in quiet voices they check the screen
next they smile obligingly and hand back my passport
remember to phone us on your return, they say
remember to phone us, they repeat

I get confused
I also want my boarding card
phone you on landing? I ask
or from my house?
they stop smiling
and my boarding card is still out of reach

the policewoman answers my question
it's up to you to find out, you know
I'll certainly be here

THE OUTERMOST SHORE

There are rocks after the headland
various sizes and the same grey colour
covering the sand of the dunes

yesterday they weren't there
stepping cautiously is difficult
even in the sunshine they're cold

the headland is already far away
the seagulls are different without their hoarse screams
space where future is memory

WAITING FOR

An ageing bus shelter with a worn-out timetable
and a faded poster advertising a disco

nobody gets on or off
metal gleams in the sunshine
the rims are well-polished

the engine's switched off
it's impossible to see the driver through the tinted windows
or work out the number of passengers

no number or terminus
I've seen it before but I don't remember when
I want to tap at the front door

without knowing where I can get off

A STRANGER

Going ashore I look around
an irrational feeling that this is home
right now and on this peninsula
where nobody knows me

once more pre-season is attractive
hardly any boats in the marina
and no cafés or shops are open

I could be living on a private road
enjoying the other houses being empty
the owners have obligations I don't know of
or they come here only in summer

they've shut off the water supply
and unplugged freezer and fridge
the chairs are empty
who's going to sit there
or maybe there

who'd be surprised if they never came back
and the darkness of the rooms was inevitable

HEADING NORTH

The next distance is snow
who provided the equipment in the trailer
not just skis and poles
also boots that fit and warm clothes?

we follow the three northbound trails
they must be quite new but although there are neither
hills nor woods we don't see anybody ahead of us
not even when using field glasses

we don't get tired or hungry
our shadows on the snow proceed as they should
no questions will be asked as long as superstition rules

CLOCKWISE

I've circled that lake at least a hundred times
anti-clockwise where the first mile is the hardest
today I turn around after a minute
to have a go at the other direction
as curious as a stranger

some trees are taller, others are lower
thickets of brambles spread without warning
roots must be tackled in a different manner
as for animals I'm confused

the lake should be the same
but there are two boats out there instead of three
who's on board?
who's on the path over there?

VIEWS

They say the mountain is an extinct volcano
which seems plausible on a day like this
although there aren't any tourists or locals

is that smoke I see or hazy dust?
maybe the earth trembles slightly

but everything's tranquil, birdsong so placid
a few yards away goats are clearing brushwood

dreaming up a different vantage point
I look for the trail I took to get here
where everything is ancient shadows

FLOOD

A lake where there was a field yesterday
and the flood's sleepless horizon

to launch a kayak
discover streams and canals
with silent currents

in more locks than you can find on a map

OBSTACLE

I've almost written about it
a door supposed to open outwards

there's some kind of obstacle
it can't be leaves
and it's too early for snowdrifts

I don't know when I last opened it
now it's important I can leave

VISIONS

All three channels flicker after the storm
so my adjustment of the aerial isn't symbolic
I try to remember its exact position
and tighten bolts before going down the ladder

there used to be a test card showing bars and circles
and notes that were useful for tuning a guitar
now it's even worse than yesterday
how many more times up and down the ladder

next twenty-year-old news updates in black and white
and much better reception than there used to be
changing channels I see colours
a city I don't recognize and a strange language and no subtitles

new networks pop up but none of the old ones
the ladder is still out there by the aerial
if I wasn't repeating myself
I'd say it isn't symbolic at all

BARRIER

The barrier between memory and words
a light wind near shadowy trees
before night's door is closed

I keep telling myself
that this is a flashback

PERFORMANCE

There are untaken seats closer to the stage but I'm in the last row
seeing them from behind I recognize a few acquaintances

the actors don't seem to mind the brightly-lit house
what's also extraordinary
is people appearing from the wings
talking and holding stuff from other productions

maybe the audience are supposed to take part
ad-libbing and tableaux passed off as art

their delivery is slow but the plot unfolds quickly

I don't remember the title until the curtain falls

MID-YEAR

The day after midsummer
there are ashes, sparks, half-burnt boughs

I last stacked a bonfire a few years ago
and only do so when I'm on my own

there's a smell of burnt photos
or negatives as I get closer

INDOORS

They're seated at the table that's usually mine
I know them so I can't be rude
what's more they smile and seem pleased to see me
and point at the free chair at the head of the table

seeing what they're having I hesitate
maybe I should order a light course and leave soon
they recommend the tasting menu with matching wines
though none of them chose it

we're soon the only diners
it's strange that there are so many new waiters
who all speak different languages
that my friends seem to know

they smile when the curtains are drawn
and lights are dimmed as the rain gains strength

TWO RIDDLES

She tells me a riddle that she claims is easy to answer
which only makes it more difficult

she smiles discreetly as if I can take my time
all the time I stare at her

I want her face to tell me the answer
I'm so curious that I want to give up but she won't let me

it's no use getting irritated
phlegm is more appropriate but hard to muster

when I finally answer it
she's disappointed and leaves at once

I follow her, knowing a riddle
that will reveal if we're different or alike

THE NEW SENDERS

Photos in the in-tray
much too regularly
the senders have unexceptional names

there's always some baffling detail
rain where I only know of sunshine
or a strange building

although the rest of the picture is clear-cut
faces are indistinct
while meeting turns into parting

DATES

All week the morning paper bears dates that are wrong
all pages are before or after today
the call centre is puzzled
they haven't received any other complaints
they must suspect I'm mad
or that my faulty copy is a one-off

the news seems to be in chronological order
also stock market fluctuation
I have doubts about the sports pages
but it appears a match was put off
I check a few TV channels to find out
if there are obsolete articles on the front page

or untimely death notices

TWO OF US

Flat and vertical sides of the head
a zigzag dorsal pattern

it's immobile in the sunshine
is it beautiful if it isn't symmetry?

stepping backwards I feel foolish
entering ignorance

no other animals
or haunting invisible birdcalls

I could be someone else's shadow
in the time it takes to clear a wilderness

THE MEETING

Who has called this meeting
we only know each other vaguely

we must reach a conclusion before we're let out
the agenda's just a draft
and most people focus on the word why

fountain pens and notebooks are produced
the woman who was smiling a lot
looks serious and slips out of her shoes

we all know each other much better now
without knowing why

CAMOUFLAGE

Something has changed
I don't know what
the people I ask don't know either

grey silence and motionless figures
they're waiting for someone
it can't be me

THE ART GALLERY

The line tells you not to get any closer
it's impossible to see if it's a photo or a painting
brushstrokes or cracks would reveal the truth

shades, dimensions, proportions
she's in a glade looking away
but is it a question of beginning or end?
and where did she come from?

no title or artist
no year to give me a clue

distant voices
the steps I hear are moving away
a mirror on the opposite wall is disguise

THERE

In the last house a window instead of yesterday's gable wall
in the front garden two new tall trees

one evening I see a light
but it may have been preset

one day a curtain
one or two looking at me
and time's intervals lose their meaning

NOW

Discreet paths
hard to follow
to this place
and somewhere else

a shadow fading among upended trees
maybe it's mine